NIGHT FLIGHT

by Kenneth Frost

MAIN STREET RAG PUBLISHING COMPANY
CHARLOTTE, NC

Cover artwork by Jonathan K. Rice

ISBN: 978-1-59948-278-1

Produced in the United States of America

Main Street Rag
PO Box 690100
Charlotte, NC 28227
www.MAINSTREETRAG.COM

ACKNOWLEDGMENTS:

The author wishes to thank the following editors and journals where these poems first appeared:

ABZ: "Chips"
The Bitter Oleander: "Bird," "Blizzard," "Burned," "Thoreau,"
    "Coring the Moon," "Lost Flutes," "Moon-Dance,"
    "Night Jockey," "Redpolls Sleeping," "Seafarer"
The Bridge: "Magnetic Resonance Imaging"
The Cape Rock: "Around the Lullaby,"
    "When the Wind Drew Up"
Confrontation: "Moon Memory"
Denver Quarterly: "Wittgenstein In Norway"
Fourteen Hills: "Stray"
Hawai'i Pacific Review: "Whispering Night"
Iodine Poetry Journal: "Mirror," "Night Flight," "The Pool"
The Mid-America Poetry Review: "In Brittle Winter,"
    "Kurt Gödel: Assumptions"
Mississippi Valley Review: "Terrorist"
Mudfish: "Half-dog," "Handkerchief Hello"
Negative Capability: "Loons On a Lake"
Nimrod: "Lightning Tree"
Occident: "Country Crossing"
Outerbridge: "Window-Washer"
The Pinch: "Assassin"
Quiddity Literary Journal: "Red Moon"
Rendevous: "Jackson Pollock"
Rosebud: "Nietzsche In Rome"
Roux: "Mandelstam—Last Stop In the Gulag"
Skidrow Penthouse: "Deserted Autumn"
The Southwest Review: "Night Patrol"
Square Lake: "Into the Humming"
The Wisconsin Review: "Thin Air"

"Window-Washer" was also included in *Outerbridge 1975-2000, A Retrospective Anthology* (2001)

for Carolyn,
Ingri, Raoul, and Christopher van der Lugt

CONTENTS

Kenneth Frost

NIGHT JOCKEY

An empty room,
a crucified fly.

The night jockey
rakes and combs
stars into bins,

bridles restless ones
with yellow ropes.

He rides meteors
bareback,

hugging them,
urging them on,

whispers
into fire's

ear.

NIETZSCHE IN ROME

Dazzled by crystals,
I unpack time.
Mirages help me,
waving their hips
like Salome wooing
the Baptist's head,
just holding
on to the
magnetic hair.
I am not here
to be
somewhere.
I am here
to be mad.

Kenneth Frost

THE POOL

I walked
into the jungle
of my laughter.
Historic creatures
full of their own weight

slipped
into the scabbard
of a glowing
pool.

      Everything
hypnotised
itself.

MIRROR

He found
a desert
in his
mirror
after
sundown
and a skull
humming
that
trapped
the night,
electric
with
sacrifice.

Kenneth Frost

BURNED

When the forest had burned down
to a cathedral

smoke
evensong

one branch kept falling
whistling to itself in the dark

an arm

raking
smoke

BIRD

The bird flaps
out of his shadow
and with a slight
shudder
the shadow streaks off,
pursuing
wild
laughter in the night.
You can hear the black
shade calling
softly to itself
for directions
in the dark,
zigzagging
hearing
the dark's voices.

The shadow joins
others calling
in the scratching
language of darkness,
writing black
into the air.

Kenneth Frost

STRAY

The angel
wings
on
fire
torch
the
dry
trees
till they
grow
thickets
of
lightning.

LIGHTNING TREE

Lightning planted
a birch tree
upsidedown.
The white tree grew whiter,
firmly rooted
in the clouds.

The branches dusted
the forest floor
so the sky
could see its reflection.
The birch flew away
in a snowstorm
with others of its kind.

Kenneth Frost

LOST FLUTES

The wind spins
weathervanes around

shrieks
at soloing
hunters' bones

Deer hold
their breath

cherry-red
in the naked
wood

BLIZZARD

Snowflakes tear
their rags deep
inside alphabets,
searching for vowels
to beat into
wilderness,

long hollow notes
finding a home
in a wolf's throat
where the wolf
before a bleeding
mirror drinks
each crack.

Kenneth Frost

THE CHASE

Coyotes float out of the trees
decked in rat coats for their full-moon
travelsong.

The flotilla bows and twists
and giggles hunger to the deer sucked
by the quicksand of newfallen snow--

these light-fingered pianothroats
trading boogie from both ends
of the keyboard, those harbor lights
trailing the guts of the full moon.

The cocaine wake of the deer's blood
grails pain to its hypnotic garden
where brain circuits are read
by a dust storm on Mars.

THE ASSASSIN

lays
one
hand
on
the
clock,
pets
its
daggers.

Kenneth Frost

TERRORIST

Angels could tell me how it feels
spending my life crawling between
the zoomlens of a reptile's eye
and a spotlight heating up
confessions in a surgical
tube that a doctor wants to stick
everywhere.
               I wonder if
a mugger carries a good luck
animal in the zoo cage
of his lead pipe, rattling
his witch doctor's spaceship
into the storm that he creates
and whether bums and rats pass in
and out of one another, one
with their underground highway.
A dead slave could tell, but won't.
Neither will this telescopic sight.

Living a life inside this sun,
crosslines that push the inner walls
of zero so it won't cave in,
I get caught in the shepherd's crook
of my own triggerfinger as
it pulls me back to life and death.

WHEN THE WIND DREW UP

it bent the light.
Grass and trees
leaked behind
the landscape.
Bushes flowered.
Reptiles glared down
through the ages.
And names hummed
a savage, hungry
lullaby.

Kenneth Frost

COUNTRY CROSSING

Too hot to handle,
the small red light
tosses itself
back and forth
to the old-style
ambulance
dinner gong.
The headlight tilts
its golden horn
along the track,
last century's
flat ladder
to paradise
the train uses
to shake the world
like prison bars.
Rock Island,
Boston and Maine,
C.P., C.P.,
boxcars cancel
themselves like mail
to violence
dislocating
the crowd of wheels
to rolling cheers
and gavels of
their guillotines.
Life being what
it is, one dreams
of revenge.
The train types
tomorrow's news
into the tape
of sheer distance.

HAYSTACK DREAMS

By good fortune
the boy was blond
and when he grew
long hair he could
hide under
its haystack.

Crows sat on his mop,
wrung him dry
in their split-tongue
language,
shrieked with delight
as their nails planted
stethoscopes
to map their adventures
in his heart.

Kenneth Frost

FOR THREE DAYS

now
just
as the clock
strikes
twelve,
the stars
begin
drumming,
drumming.
"It's all right,"
I keep
saying.
Then,
a left foot
burning
drops
through the air
of sleep.

THIN AIR

I.

The Dalai Lama gets
yak butter rubbed
into his skin to bind
sweat with the milk
of heaven.

Blue sky must reek exile
in a boy
although he has no wrinkles
and remains young longer
because he is a god
ducking in and out
of castles of the flesh
by ratholes underground.

II.

An ever-lengthening
spiral
distances him from
his body,

becomes so long
all chance of return
is lost.

The parabola wobbles,
the peak
curves off in space.

The echoes, shorter,
live in a previous life.

Kenneth Frost

HALF DOG,

half coyote,
half man
rode a white horse
in his sleep.
He could hear
the Dog Star
vacuum up
the hoofbeats.
He stopped the dream
short,
his iridescent horse
kicked the dream
and ate
the sweet grass
sprouted.

MOON MEMORY

I.

Messenger
        liquor of light
let the walleyed
moons of the whale
                his whole bulk
glow memory

II.

a blackjack bowing
tapping the palm
           of the night air
measuring
        this tropic beach
with the dance step
of compass points
            puppetry
on his tail fins

III.

dreams
        flashing their teeth
encircle him
till he retreats
          from the sixth day

Kenneth Frost

INTO THE HUMMING

My bones are brittle as glass.
Can I look into them,

into the humming tunnel,
the hollow core,

to hear my heart
and see the moon,

a maze of moons
beating, beating?

A heartbeat walks
on the moon's plague of eggs,

a hangover of drums
fits each step.

MAGNETIC RESONANCE IMAGING

It's delicate.
I could have named
galactic clusters formed like it
Veronica's Veil
of ice.

In this magnetic cave
hydrogen atoms sing
water to flesh,
a rotting face.

In total darkness
water has found
itself.

Kenneth Frost

RAINY NIGHT VOICES

Nothing is tight enough
to keep voices
in rainy nights from speaking
low voices, hoarse voices,
almost undersea voices.
You cannot hear them

until hush-hush
inhales the mind
in its slow
groaning
and cracks open like a bone
releasing winged, smiling creatures.

WINDOW-WASHER

Lowering
the lifeboat of
our platform from
the roof each day,
I sort of know
what escapees
of shipwrecks feel
looking in
at the portholes
like peeping toms.
I concentrate
on soaping up
and shining glass
so the roulette
wheel of sunlight
won't skid my head
around its track.
As I move down,
sideways and down,
I read my life
in the headlines
my printing press
is slapping out:
"They didn't know
that he was there
till he was not."

Kenneth Frost

HANDKERCHIEF HELLO

My senile aunt
waves her hand like a handkerchief hello
to the old lady
who comes to the mirror's castle window-frame
each night and waves
herself into her fingertips goodbye
before one of them climbs, hand over hand,
the stairway to
the mountain peak of sleep.

Who speaks the caressing command?

Stirred around the golden
whirlpool of a pendulum,
I am contemplated by
my own motion
inward.
I never knew
that I would know such peace.

A drop of water
as it hits, explodes
into a crown
emptying itself.

SEAFARER

He sits
in the
crowsnest
of the
needle,
stitches
foam
together
to make
lace
for the
black
muscles
of his
heart.

Kenneth Frost

WITTGENSTEIN IN NORWAY

The sun loses
control of day
on the lake ice,
banging a drum
with a blackjack
till a mad dog
crouches beside me
stretching
his eyeteeth
in icicles.

A single cloud,
a damaged hemisphere,
floats over my head.
I think alone,
sing alone,
eat and talk alone,
wear the smile
twelve-year-olds
smile,
while my fellow
logician,
Bach, instructs
the glass harmonica
of the dog's teeth.

IN BRITTLE WINTER

The shaman sun
   whirls,
      flashes and flaps

his tin feathers,
   catches
      a last glimpse

in shattered mirrors,
   disappears
      into a dream.

Kenneth Frost

MANDELSTAM—
LAST STOP IN THE GULAG

The wind alone tunes a bare twig.
Today the wind feels like Orpheus.
He needs a head, a bird's head.
The shrike, airing a hook talks
like a hunchback fallen
into the white world that crowds
mirrors out of glaze. All afternoon
air is cutting diamonds—
manias of facets look
for the right sun to search
the coldest memory in light.
The dead live snowflake moments
on the gangplank of my black tongue
as I forage for a dead king's
dinner alone eating blind eyes.

REDPOLLS SLEEPING

A white amnesia.
The field twitters
restless warning
of night floating above
on ticking paws.

The Arctic thinks
in trembling chords
like barbed wire
with the wind counting
its steel knots.

Ghosts on the loose,
can you hear
coral orchards
pour hypnosis
through the wind?

These little finches sleep in snow tunnels to keep warm,
and even at night they restlessly twitter to one another.

Kenneth Frost

NIGHT PATROL

I walk on water yet high-step—
majorette as nightmare running in mud
with each step blaring like a band.
Sounds vibrate in my jawbone
like angels embedded in a swamp.
The heart jumps over the moon
time and again trying to teach
a cow to be a hundred sheep
so I can rise and sleepwalk in
animal ancestors with brazen eyes,
soft-colored and padded as armored vests.

WHISPERING NIGHT

The night whispers
to abandoned wells.
The spirits in them,
standing on tiptoes,
keeping their heads
above water,
complain of lost ills.
Stars hear them,
they shift positions.
The Bowman drops
his bow and listens.
Beasts lower their heads,
staring out of the tops
of their eyes.
What do they hear,
these deep
exiles of grief?

Kenneth Frost

DESERTED AUTUMN

Where empty rooms
search for survivors
in a cracked window,
how could he hear
the leaves crumble
in their deserted veins?

The red, purple and gold
diseased splendors
shake their chronometers.
Voices rattle the tin
cups of the leaves,
memories

begging for blood.
A phalanx
of blanched draculas
surges forward
to the dead drum
in a dog's throat.

KURT GÖDEL: ASSUMPTIONS

Time bends around the universe
in curving lines.

Change is an illusion,
infinite sets exist,
you can go backward
and forward in time.

My death certificate
will state I died
of malnutrition.

I took everything about me
with me

except what Newton says:

By the ultimate ratio
of evanescent quantities
is to be understood
the ratio of quantities
not before they vanish
nor after they vanish,
but with which they vanish.

Kenneth Frost

LOONS ON A LAKE

My dog keeps twisting her head
back and forth like a doorknob
to open up the emptiness
of loons crying on the lake.
She understands this is a code.

If mathematical logic
had a song, somehow
it rightly placed itself
in gamebirds better
at swimming than most fish

with vocables
that haunt their flesh.
Extraterrestrial life
is answering terrestrial life.
No one should be here or there.

FULL MOON,

whose light
do you
whittle
yourself
by
that you groan
at
your
harvest?

Kenneth Frost

JACKSON POLLOCK

What is it I
am looking for?
Paul Valery
said, "One does not
finish a poem;
in the end, one
abandons it,"
but I'll bet Bach
could have written
all of his fugues
at once--I race
that labyrinth
through my childhood
in atom tracks
and galaxies
that drift flotsam
of light behind.
That ought to prove
that a dripstick--
my blindman's cane,
that one-legged
tapdancer and
dull machete--
is quick with light,
but all it proves
is deepsea fish,
blind maharajahs
sitting under
sunflower silk
umbrellas of

outmoded light,
simply explode
if they rise up.
The speed of light
haunts the abstract,
my absolute.

Kenneth Frost

CHIPS

A man
grew fat
on a diet of Botticelli:

potato chips
flaked off
The Birth of Venus.

He especially liked
annunciation chips.
Angel's wing

made his mouth water
with the taste
of peacock eyes.

In the dead wing
of the museum,
you can still hear

his ravenous mouth.

MOON-DANCE

On clear nights,
spiders hear
stars talk
to stones.

The stones lift
their heavy
lids and blink back.

Their tutu
legs *en pointe,*
spiders circle

in tighter
and tighter zeroes,
drilling
the shining
ground.

Kenneth Frost

CORING THE MOON

The full moon has a hole in it,
right in the center.
If you look closely,
you can see a long tunnel
and dark creatures
traveling through it.
Then they drop out of sight.
Do they fall into a trap,
a black hole, or nothing?
Coyotes run in circles,
mad for the nothing of the moon.
They try on their ghosts
in the moon's dressing room.
Owls become raucous
and tear their spirits limb from limb.
The hole passes with a long howl,
and men and raccoons and deer
come out of the woods,
moonstruck.

THOREAU

Coyotes pad
on the pine needles
and bend midnight
to a breeze
while their slight smile buries
hunger
like old pharaohs
in their eyeteeth.

Are these the bright
hollows whip-poor-wills
slide into songs,
the famishing haloes
circulating
over the sleep
the minnow fans
deep in his mirror
flickering dreams
with his slow fins?

Kenneth Frost

AROUND THE LULLABY

The black bear sleeps
around the lullaby
of his heart slowed
to hovering
its black sail.

Nerve-ends
to an ash tree,
a crow listens
to his soft undertow
of blood.

Light leaves the late
afternoon.
The field asks
nothing from its crow's-foot
language of snow.

RED MOON

A crow
pulls
his black
cloak
over
his
shoulders
and sinks
deeper
into
the red
quarter
moon.

Kenneth Frost

NIGHT FLIGHT

The mind
    steps on
        a crack
    vibrating
cello notes
their liquors
      leak
        blind alleys
    midnight's
tree.